Spotlight on

Farm Animals

Tim Wood

Franklin Watts

London · New York · Sydney · Toronto

© 1988 Franklin Watts

Franklin Watts
12a Golden Square
London W1

First published in the USA by
Franklin Watts Inc.
387 Park Avenue South
New York, N.Y. 10016

Franklin Watts Australia
14 Mars Road
Lane Cove
NSW 2066

Phototypeset by Keyspools
Limited
Printed in Hong Kong

UK ISBN: 0 86313 658 3
US ISBN: 0-531-10543-1
Library of Congress Catalog
Card Number: 87-51477

Illustrations:
Christopher Forsey
Hayward Art Group
N. E. Middleton

Photographs:
Australian Information Service
ISA Poultry Services Ltd
David Jefferis
Milk Marketing Board
Chris Fairclough
ZEFA

Design:
Janet King
David Jefferis

Technical consultant:
Tony Jefferis, Manager of
Knighton Wood Farm

Note: A number of the
illustrations in this book originally
appeared in *Farm Animals*, A First
Look Book.

Contents

Animals on the farm

Animals were first tamed for use on farms about 10,000 years ago.

Animals provided meat, eggs and milk. They also provided wool for cloth and skins for leather. Some animals were used by farmers to carry or pull heavy loads.

A French farm about 500 years ago.

Ancestors of farm animals

The ancestors of modern farm animals were wild creatures. Careful breeding may have changed their size or shape, and made them suitable for their job on the farm.

Wild goose

Wild duck

Mountain sheep

Wild boar

Aurochs

Jungle fowl

These are the ancestors of some of today's farm animals.

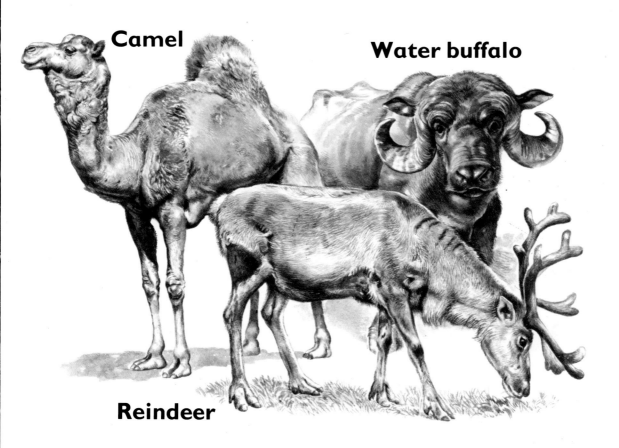

Camel

Water buffalo

Reindeer

Some useful animals from around the world.

Many different animals are used by farmers around the world. Camels carry loads in desert areas. Water buffalo pull ploughs in India and Asia. Reindeer meat is eaten in Scandinavia.

7

Cattle

Beef cattle are kept for their meat. The best breeds, such as the Aberdeen Angus, are heavy animals. They have big hindquarters, where the tastiest meat comes from. Dairy cattle, such as Jerseys and Friesians, are kept for their milk. They are milked twice a day, morning and evening. The milk is released from the cow's udder through four teats.

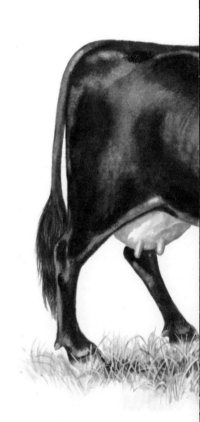

Friesians – popular dairy cattle.

Aberdeen Angus

Jersey

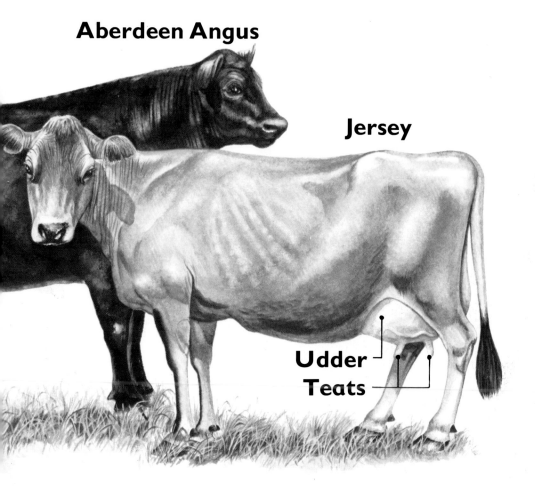

Udder
Teats

9

Calves and milking

A cow's body changes the grass she eats into milk. Sometimes farmers give their cows extra food like hay to improve the amount and quality of the milk.

A milking machine in action. A cow can produce up to 39 pints (22 l) of milk a day.

Cows give birth to their first calves when they are about three years old.

A cow starts to produce milk when she gives birth to her first calf. Soon after they are born, calves are taken from their mothers and fed on other food. Cows are then milked regularly for about ten months. After that, the amount of milk a cow gives drops until her next calf is born.

Sheep

There are two main types of sheep. Highland sheep are tough and can survive on cold, bare hillsides. But they have poor quality wool and give birth to fewer lambs.

Highland sheep eat heather, small plants and grass.

Lowland sheep. Sheep have no top front teeth. They crop the grass by tearing at it.

Lowland sheep have better quality wool but need shelter and good grass. Australia and New Zealand are the world's largest sheep-producing countries. Australian sheep produce fine wool. New Zealand sheep are raised for meat.

Lambing and shearing

Sheep-shearers in Australia using electric clippers to remove the woolly coat.

Springtime is lambing time. The lambs raised for meat are sold when they are about three months old. Summer is shearing time. In warmer weather sheep shed their fleeces naturally in untidy lumps. The shearers clip off the fleece in one piece before this happens.

Lowland ewes often have twins, sometimes triplets.

Lambs and their mothers recognize each other by smell and call.

Pigs

Pigs provide pork, bacon and ham. Pigs used for meat are kept indoors so that they put on weight quickly. Pigs kept for breeding stay out of doors.

A Saddleback pig cooling down in a mud bath.

A sow feeding her litter.

Pigs are clean animals but they cannot sweat so they roll in mud to keep cool. Female pigs, called sows, have two or three litters of piglets a year, each one with nine or more babies.

17

Goats

Goats are very sure-footed. They do well in mountainous areas.

Goats are popular in hot countries where the grass is too poor for sheep and cattle. They produce milk, and some, like the Angora goat, have fine, silky hair which is used as mohair for sweaters.

A goat gives about 5 pints (3 l) of milk a day. In many countries people keep one or two goats to provide their family with milk. Goats are good climbers and will eat almost anything. It is important to tie them up firmly!

As well as grass, goats will eat weeds, tree bark, even thistles!

Horses

Horses used to do the work that tractors do today. Draught horses were specially bred to be strong and heavy. They pulled ploughs, heavy carts and other farm machines.

Farmers on horseback rounding up sheep.

Draught horses ploughing.

Horses are still used on large farms in Australia and America. Farmers ride round the farm looking for any sheep or cattle which have strayed from the herd. They round up the animals, count them and drive them to market.

21

Chickens

Chicken Duck

Goose Turkey

The eggs of
farm birds.
These are half
life size.

Birds raised for meat are kept in huge chicken houses. They are fed a rich diet and killed within two months. Egg-laying birds are kept in houses called batteries where the food and light are controlled to encourage them to lay eggs.

Chickens which peck about in the open are called free-range. They lay fewer eggs than battery hens.

Battery hens. Their eggs roll from their cages into collecting trays.

23

Turkeys, geese and ducks

Chicken

Turkey

Duck

Goose

The feet of farm birds. The ones which can swim have webbed feet.

Turkeys are kept in large numbers in big wire enclosures. They are popular food at Christmas and on Thanksgiving Day in America. Turkeys need careful looking after as they can pick up diseases. Ducks and geese give eggs and meat. Their feathers are used to stuff pillows and quilts.

Turkeys used to be huge birds, but today's breeds are smaller so they can fit into modern ovens.

Ducks and geese are water birds.

Farm animal breeds

Here are some breeds of farm animals.

Merino
Fine wool.

Scottish Blackface
Good meat and wool.

Oxford Down   Border Leicester
Both give good meat and wool.

Guernsey
Gives rich, creamy milk.

North American Friesian
Gives lots of milk.

Charolais
A French beef breed.

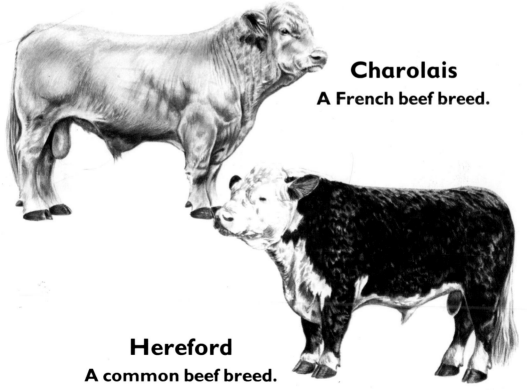

Hereford
A common beef breed.

New breeds of animals can be
made by mating different animals.
A mule is a cross between a horse
and a donkey.
Donkeys and mules carry people
and their loads in many countries.

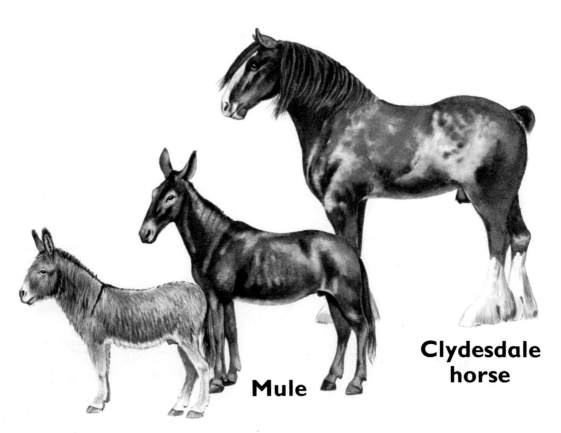

Donkey

Mule

Clydesdale
horse

Rhode Island Red
A good egg-layer.

White Leghorn
A good egg-layer.

Light Sussex
**A good egg-layer but also
kept for its meat.**

Saddleback
**Kept for bacon
and pork.**

Gloucester Old Spot
One of the oldest breeds of pig.

Farm animal facts

The auroch, ancestor of cattle breeds, was a huge beast. A full-grown bull was 6.5 ft (2 m) high at the shoulders. The last auroch died in Poland in 1627.

A New Zealand farmer holds the record for the largest number of sheep sheared in a working day – 804 in 9 hours!

A highland sheep proved how tough it was by surviving for 50 days buried in snow on a Scottish farm in 1978.

Pigs are used in France to sniff out truffles, a type of underground mushroom used in dishes in expensive restaurants. One problem is that pigs like them so much that the keepers have to work hard to stop the pigs eating the truffles as soon as they find them.

In 1984 there were about 4,500,000,000 chickens in the world – about one for every person.

The world egg-laying record is held by a White Leghorn who laid 371 eggs in 364 days. The biggest ever hen's egg was also laid by a White Leghorn. The monster egg weighed in at a staggering 454 grams (16 oz)!

The highest number of piglets ever born in one litter is 34.

Roast goose was the favourite meal of Queen Elizabeth I of England.

The goose is the longest living of all domestic birds. The oldest known goose died in 1976, aged 49 years and 8 months.

Glossary

Here is the meaning of some of the words used in this book:

Ancestors

Members of a group of animals which lived a long time ago.

Battery

A large hen house filled with wire cages. The food and light are controlled to encourage the birds to lay eggs.

Breed

One of the varieties of a particular animal. Jersey and Friesian are two breeds of cattle.

Breeding

Keeping animals to produce young. Farmers use specially chosen animals to change or develop a breed.

Ewe

An adult female sheep. An adult male is a ram. A baby sheep is a lamb.

Free-range

The name given to chickens which are allowed to grow up in the open air, rather than being kept in battery cages.

Litter

A family of baby animals born at one time.

Milking machine

A machine for milking cows. Special tubes are attached to the cows' teats in the milking parlour. The milk is sucked gently from the udders and pumped into containers.

Shearing

Clipping off the fleece of a sheep in one piece. Shearing used to be done with hand clippers but now these are powered by electricity.

Index